LET'S PLAY! LITTLE CHAMPS

T-BALL

RYAN JAMES

NORWOOD HOUSE PRESS

Library of Congress Cataloging-in-Publication Data

Names: James, Ryan.
Title: T-ball / Ryan James.
Description: Buffalo, NY : Norwood House Press, 2025. | Series: Let's play! little champs | Includes glossary and index.
Identifiers: ISBN 9781684502233 (pbk.) | ISBN 9781684502240 (library bound) | ISBN 9781684502257 (ebook)
Subjects: LCSH: T-ball--Juvenile literature.
Classification: LCC GV881.5 J359 2025 | DDC 796.357'8--dc23

Published in 2025 by
Norwood House Press
2544 Clinton Street
Buffalo, NY 14224

Designer: Ocean Books
Editor: Kim Thompson

Photo credits: Cover, p. 1 Digital Media Pro/Shutterstock.com; pp. 5, 14, 15, 19 Jonathan Novak/Shutterstock.com; p. 6 Brian Eichhorn/Shutterstock.com; p. 8 tammykayphoto/Shutterstock.com; p. 9 Volodymyr TVERDOKHLIB/Shutterstock.com; p. 11 Monkey Business Images; p. 12 Jeep Thrower/Shutterstock.com; p. 13 Kim Murrell/ Shutterstock.com; p. 16 Lost_in_the_Midwest/Shutterstock.com; p. 17 Stuart Monk/Shutterstock.com; p. 18 Steve Bower/Shutterstock.com; p. 21 Prostock-studio/ Shutterstock.com

Printed in the United States of America

CPSIA compliance information: Batch #CW25NHP: For further information contact Norwood House Press at 1-800-237-9932.

TABLE OF CONTENTS

What Is T-Ball?

T-ball is a fun game. It is like baseball, but for younger kids. The ball is not **pitched**. Instead, players hit the ball off a **tee**.

The Uniform

A jersey shows the team colors. Pants protect a player's legs during slides and falls.

Special shoes called cleats have small spikes on the bottom. They help players run on dirt and grass.

The player who is batting must wear a helmet to protect their head.

The Field

The field has first base, second base, third base, and home plate. The tee is at home plate. Lines show where to run and where the **outfield** begins.

Rules of the Game

There are no **strikeouts** in T-ball. Batters keep trying until they get a hit.

After a hit, the player runs around the bases. They try to get to all the bases without being **tagged** by a player on the other team.

A game has three or four **innings**. Each team bats once in each inning. All players get a chance to hit and **field**.

Positions on the Team

One team is at bat. Players hitting off the tee are called batters. Players running around the bases are called runners.

The other team is on the field. Fielders try to catch or pick up the ball after it is hit. They make an out when they tag a runner or throw the ball to a base before the runner gets there.

The **catcher** is part of the fielding team. They stand behind home plate to catch balls that are missed. They can also help make an out.

The pitcher is also part of the fielding team. They do not pitch the ball, but they stand near the pitcher's mound. They catch or pick up balls that are hit up the middle of the field.

How to Be Game-Ready

Players should eat healthy foods like fruits, vegetables, and lean meats. They should drink plenty of water. Getting enough sleep gives them energy to run and play.

GLOSSARY

catcher (KACH-ur): the player who stands behind home plate to catch balls that are not hits and to help their team field balls

field (feeld): to catch or pick up batted balls, throw batted balls to teammates, and try to make outs on players from the opposite team

innings (IN-ingz): parts of a T-ball game in which each team gets a turn at bat

outfield (OUT-feeld): the part of a T-ball field that is beyond the bases and inside the foul lines

pitched (pichd): thrown by a pitcher for batters to hit

strikeouts (STRIKE-outs): outs in baseball that happen when a batter gets three strikes, or fails to hit the ball three times

tagged (tagd): touched a runner with the ball to make an out

tee (tee): an adjustable post on which a ball is placed for batting

THINKING QUESTIONS

1. What are the parts of a T-ball player's uniform?
2. Why do fielders have an important position?
3. What is the difference between T-ball and regular baseball?
4. Why do T-ball players need to eat healthy foods?
5. What qualities do you think a good T-ball player has?

INDEX

ABOUT THE AUTHOR

Ryan James lives in the western part of North Carolina with his rescue dog Bailey. As a child, he would search for creepy crawlies as he hiked through the forest near his house. When he's not on the hiking or biking trail, he is cheering on his favorite baseball and football teams.